FRANK LLOYD WRIGHT

1867–1959

Frank Lloyd Wright is recognized worldwide as one of the greatest architects of the twentieth century. He started his life soon after the American Civil War and concluded his journey during the dawn of the space age. His work heralded a new thinking in architecture, using innovation in design and engineering made possible by newly developed technology and materials. His creative ability extended far beyond the border of architecture to graphic design, furniture, art glass, textiles, and decorative elements for the home. His philosophy, represented in these buildings, reflects timeless and relevant ideas about sustainability, innovation, democratic design, and ultimately, what American architecture could and should be.

FRANK LLOYD WRIGHT AT DESK

Organic simplicity
might be seen
producing significant
character in the
harmonious order
we call Nature:
all around, beauty
in growing things.
None insignificant.

_____

FRANK LLOYD WRIGHT

YUCCA PLANT ABSTRACTION
EUGENE MASSELINK, 1960

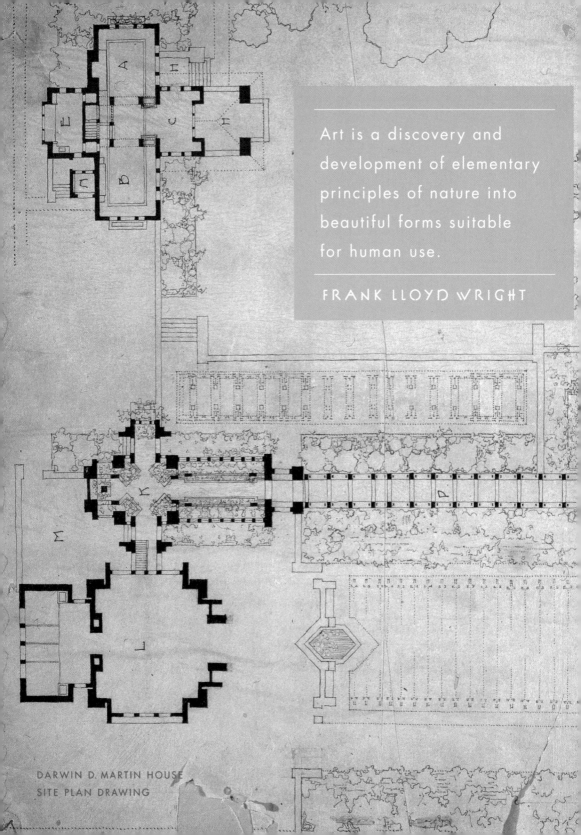

Art is a discovery and
development of elementary
principles of nature into
beautiful forms suitable
for human use.

FRANK LLOYD WRIGHT

DARWIN D. MARTIN HOUSE
SITE PLAN DRAWING

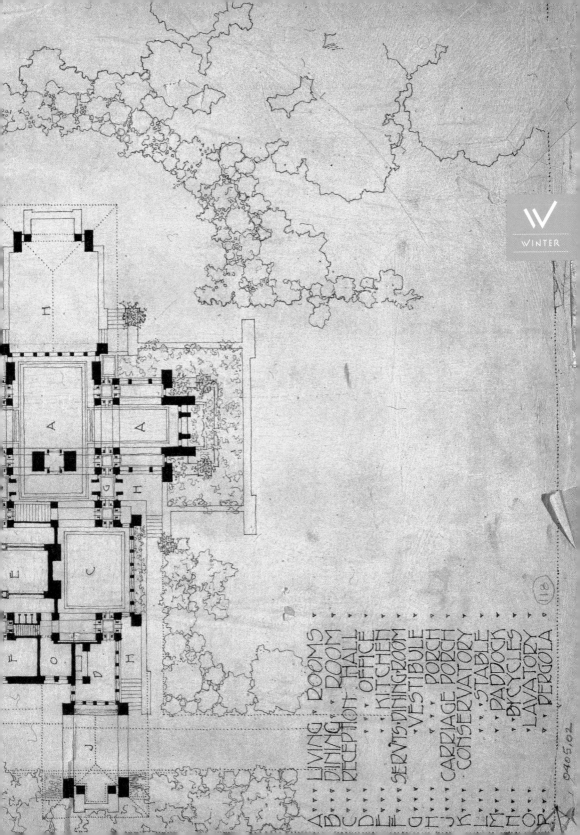

A · LIVING · ROOMS
B · DINING · ROOM
C · RECEPTION · HALL
D · OFFICE
E · KITCHEN
F · SERV'TS·DINING ROOM
G · VESTIBULE
H · PORCH
I · CARRIAGE PORCH
J · CONSERVATORY
K · STABLE
L · PADDOCK
M · BICYCLES
N · LAVATORY
O · PERGOLA

0405.02

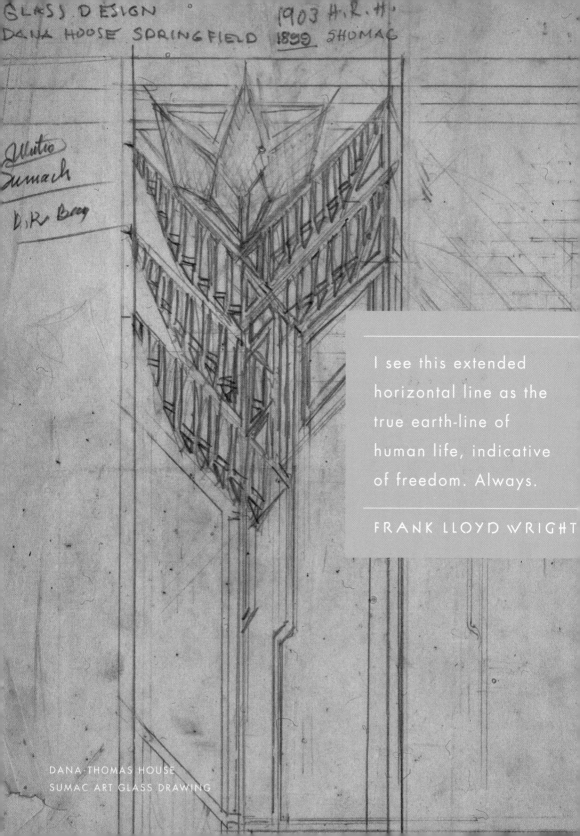

GLASS DESIGN
DANA HOUSE SPRINGFIELD 1899 SHUMAC

1903 H.R.H.

Matte
Sumach

D.R. Bry

I see this extended
horizontal line as the
true earth-line of
human life, indicative
of freedom. Always.

FRANK LLOYD WRIGHT

DANA-THOMAS HOUSE
SUMAC ART GLASS DRAWING

ART GLASS IN BREAKFAST NOOK AT DANA-THOMAS HOUSE
PHOTOGRAPH COPYRIGHT DOUG CARR
COURTESY OF THE DANA-THOMAS HOUSE FOUNDATION

TIGER LILIES ABSTRACTION
EUGENE MASSELINK 1958

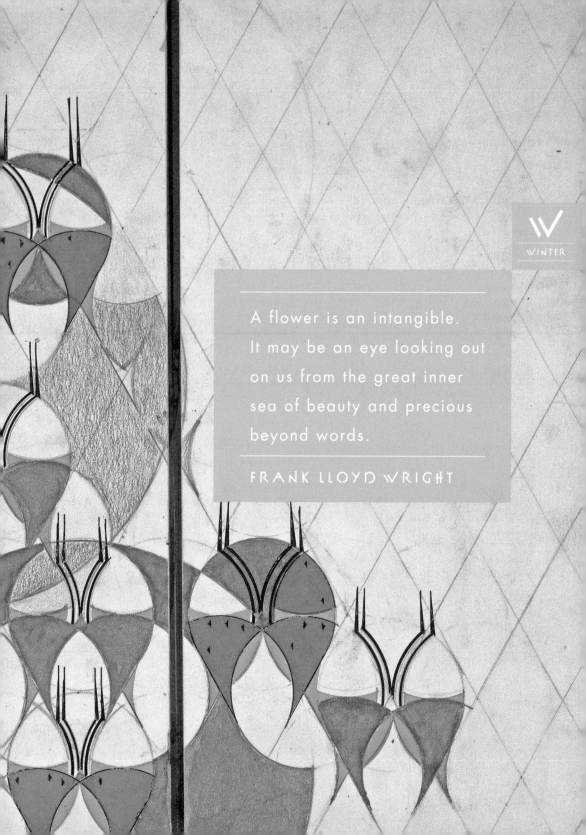

WINTER

A flower is an intangible.
It may be an eye looking out
on us from the great inner
sea of beauty and precious
beyond words.

FRANK LLOYD WRIGHT

PLANT PROFILE

Plant Name: Description:

Date
Planted: Quantity
Planted:

Date
Germinated: Quantity
Germinated:

Care
Instructions:

Known
Problems:

Projected
Height: Projected
Season Length:

How To
Harvest: Amount
Harvested:

Additional
Notes:

Plant Name: Description:

Date
Planted: Quantity
Planted:

Date
Germinated: Quantity
Germinated:

Care
Instructions:

Known
Problems:

Projected
Height: Projected
Season Length:

How To
Harvest: Amount
Harvested:

Additional
Notes:

PLANT PROFILE

Plant Name: Description:

Date
Planted: Quantity
Planted:

Date
Germinated: Quantity
Germinated:

Care
Instructions:

Known
Problems:

Projected
Height: Projected
Season Length:

How To
Harvest: Amount
Harvested:

Additional
Notes:

WINTER

Plant Name: Description:

Date
Planted: Quantity
Planted:

Date
Germinated: Quantity
Germinated:

Care
Instructions:

Known
Problems:

Projected
Height: Projected
Season Length:

How To
Harvest: Amount
Harvested:

Additional
Notes:

PLANT PROFILE

Plant Name:

Description:

Date
Planted:

Quantity
Planted:

Date
Germinated:

Quantity
Germinated:

Care
Instructions:

Known
Problems:

Projected
Height:

Projected
Season Length:

How To
Harvest:

Amount
Harvested:

Additional
Notes:

Plant Name:

Description:

Date
Planted:

Quantity
Planted:

Date
Germinated:

Quantity
Germinated:

Care
Instructions:

Known
Problems:

Projected
Height:

Projected
Season Length:

How To
Harvest:

Amount
Harvested:

Additional
Notes:

PLANT PROFILE

Plant Name: Description:

Date   Quantity
Planted: Planted:

Date   Quantity
Germinated: Germinated:

Care
Instructions:

Known
Problems:

Projected   Projected
Height: Season Length:

How To   Amount
Harvest: Harvested:

Additional
Notes:

Plant Name: Description:

Date   Quantity
Planted: Planted:

Date   Quantity
Germinated: Germinated:

Care
Instructions:

Known
Problems:

Projected   Projected
Height: Season Length:

How To   Amount
Harvest: Harvested:

Additional
Notes:

PLANT PROFILE

Plant Name: Description:

Date
Planted: Quantity
Planted:

Date
Germinated: Quantity
Germinated:

Care
Instructions:

Known
Problems:

Projected
Height: Projected
Season Length:

How To
Harvest: Amount
Harvested:

Additional
Notes:

Plant Name: Description:

Date
Planted: Quantity
Planted:

Date
Germinated: Quantity
Germinated:

Care
Instructions:

Known
Problems:

Projected
Height: Projected
Season Length:

How To
Harvest: Amount
Harvested:

Additional
Notes:

PLANT PROFILE

Plant Name: Description:

Date   Quantity
Planted: Planted:

Date   Quantity
Germinated: Germinated:

Care   W
Instructions: WINTER

Known
Problems:

Projected   Projected
Height: Season Length:

How To   Amount
Harvest: Harvested:

Additional
Notes:

Plant Name: Description:

Date   Quantity
Planted: Planted:

Date   Quantity
Germinated: Germinated:

Care
Instructions:

Known
Problems:

Projected   Projected
Height: Season Length:

How To   Amount
Harvest: Harvested:

Additional
Notes:

PLANT PROFILE

Plant Name:

Description:

Date
Planted:

Quantity
Planted:

Date
Germinated:

Quantity
Germinated:

Care
Instructions:

Known
Problems:

Projected
Height:

Projected
Season Length:

How To
Harvest:

Amount
Harvested:

Additional
Notes:

Plant Name:

Description:

Date
Planted:

Quantity
Planted:

Date
Germinated:

Quantity
Germinated:

Care
Instructions:

Known
Problems:

Projected
Height:

Projected
Season Length:

How To
Harvest:

Amount
Harvested:

Additional
Notes:

PLANT PROFILE

Plant Name: Description:

Date   Quantity
Planted: Planted:

Date   Quantity
Germinated: Germinated:

Care
Instructions:

Known
Problems:

Projected   Projected
Height: Season Length:

How To   Amount
Harvest: Harvested:

Additional
Notes:

Plant Name: Description:

Date   Quantity
Planted: Planted:

Date   Quantity
Germinated: Germinated:

Care
Instructions:

Known
Problems:

Projected   Projected
Height: Season Length:

How To   Amount
Harvest: Harvested:

Additional
Notes:

Notes:

Notes:

Notes:

Notes:

GARDEN PLAN

GARDEN PLAN

GARDEN PLAN

GARDEN PLAN

WINTER

GARDEN PLAN

GARDEN PLAN

WINTER

WINTER TO DO LIST

○   DATE

○   DATE

○   DATE

○   DATE

○   DATE

○   DATE

○   DATE

○   DATE

○   DATE

○   DATE

○   DATE

○   DATE

○   DATE

○   DATE

○   DATE

○   DATE

○   DATE

○   DATE

○   DATE

○   DATE

○   DATE

○   DATE

○   DATE

○   DATE

○   DATE

○   DATE

○   DATE

○   DATE

○   DATE

○   DATE

○   DATE

○   DATE

○   DATE

○   DATE

W
WINTER

WINTER TO DO LIST

○   DATE

○   DATE

○   DATE

○   DATE

○   DATE

○   DATE

○   DATE

○   DATE

○   DATE

○   DATE

○   DATE

○   DATE

○   DATE

○   DATE

○   DATE

○   DATE

WINTER TO DO LIST

- ○   DATE
- ○   DATE
- ○   DATE

W
WINTER

- ○   DATE
- ○   DATE
- ○   DATE
- ○   DATE
- ○   DATE
- ○   DATE
- ○   DATE
- ○   DATE
- ○   DATE
- ○   DATE
- ○   DATE
- ○   DATE
- ○   DATE
- ○   DATE

MONTH / YEAR

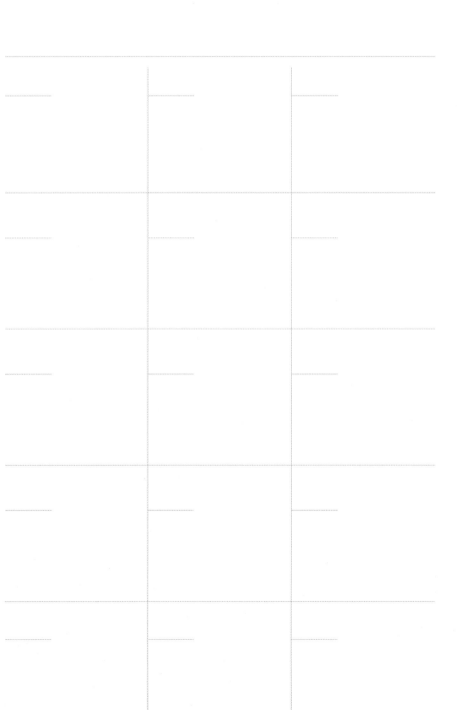

MONTH / YEAR

WINTER CALENDAR

WINTER

MONTH / YEAR

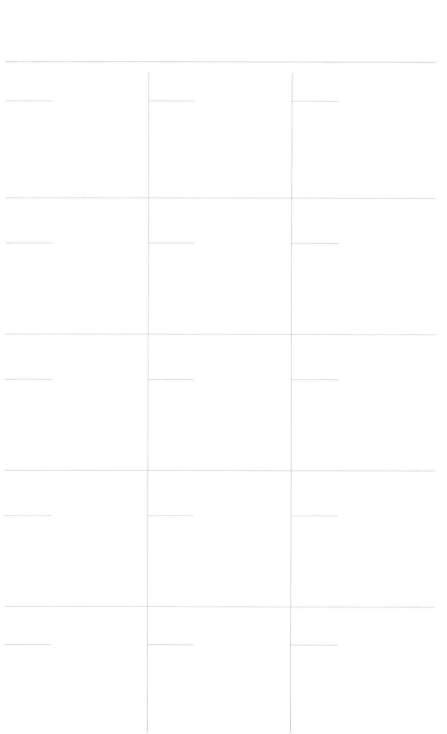

WINTER CLIMATE DATA WORTH NOTING

DATE

DATE

DATE

DATE

DATE

DATE

DATE

DATE

DATE

WINTER CLIMATE DATA WORTH NOTING

DATE

DATE

WINTER

DATE

DATE

DATE

DATE

DATE

DATE

DATE

PESTS & PROBLEMS

DATE	PLANT	PROBLEM

PESTS & PROBLEMS

TREATMENT	DID IT WORK?

Study nature, love nature,
stay close to nature.
It will never fail you.

FRANK LLOYD WRIGHT

SP

SPRING

L L DOAN HOUSE ABSTRACTION
EUGENE MASSELINK 1957

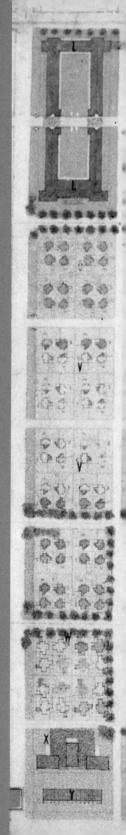

An organic form grows its structure
out of conditions as a plant grows
out of soil... both unfold similarly
from within.

FRANK LLOYD WRIGHT

MODEL QUARTER SECTION
CITY RESIDENTIAL LAND DEVELOPMENT, CHICAGO, IL

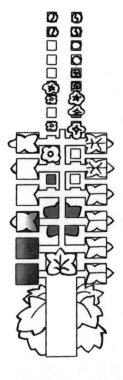

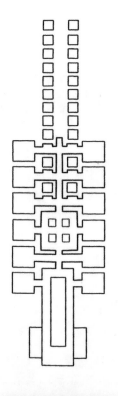

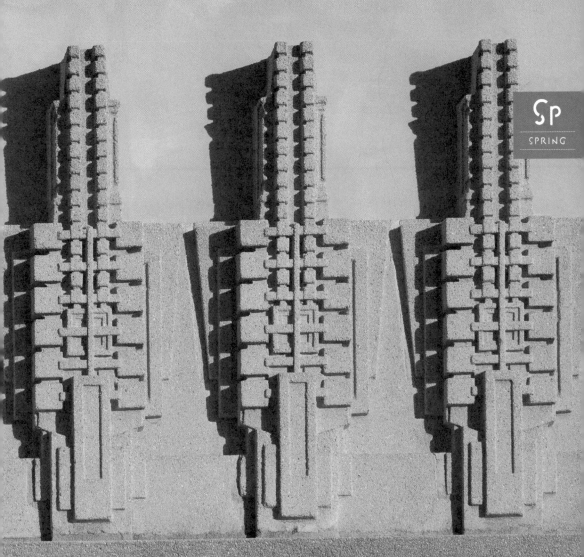

You might say that Nature is
the God of the architect.

FRANK LLOYD WRIGHT

LEFT: HOLLYHOCK ILLUSTRATIONS FROM FRANK LLOYD WRIGHT FOR KIDS BY KATH-
LEEN THORNE-THOMSEN PUBLISHED BY THE CHICAGO REVIEW PRESS. COURTESY OF
THE AUTHOR.
RIGHT: HOLLYHOCK HOUSE FRIEZE, PHOTOGRAPHY © QUINTIN LAKE

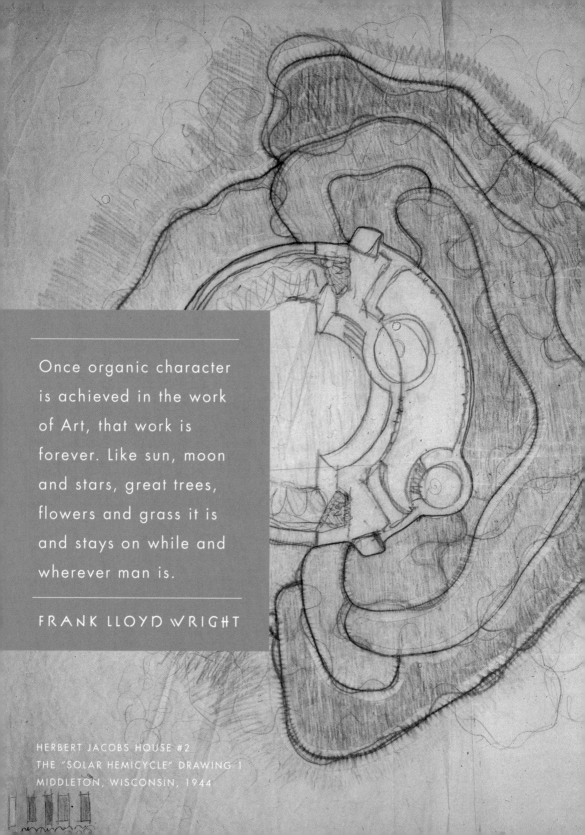

Once organic character
is achieved in the work
of Art, that work is
forever. Like sun, moon
and stars, great trees,
flowers and grass it is
and stays on while and
wherever man is.

FRANK LLOYD WRIGHT

SP

SPRING

HERBERT JACOBS HOUSE #2
THE "SOLAR HEMICYCLE" DRAWING 2
MIDDLETON, WISCONSIN, 1944

PLANT PROFILE

Plant Name: Description:

Date
Planted: Quantity
Planted:

Date
Germinated: Quantity
Germinated:

Care
Instructions:

Known
Problems:

Projected
Height: Projected
Season Length:

How To
Harvest: Amount
Harvested:

Additional
Notes:

Plant Name: Description:

Date
Planted: Quantity
Planted:

Date
Germinated: Quantity
Germinated:

Care
Instructions:

Known
Problems:

Projected
Height: Projected
Season Length:

How To
Harvest: Amount
Harvested:

Additional
Notes:

PLANT PROFILE

Plant Name: .... Description: ....

Date
Planted: ....

Quantity
Planted: ....

Date
Germinated: ....

Quantity
Germinated: ....

Care
Instructions: ....

Known
Problems: ....

Projected
Height: ....

Projected
Season Length: ....

How To
Harvest: ....

Amount
Harvested: ....

Additional
Notes: ....

Plant Name: .... Description: ....

Date
Planted: ....

Quantity
Planted: ....

Date
Germinated: ....

Quantity
Germinated: ....

Care
Instructions: ....

Known
Problems: ....

Projected
Height: ....

Projected
Season Length: ....

How To
Harvest: ....

Amount
Harvested: ....

Additional
Notes: ....

PLANT PROFILE

Plant Name: Description:

Date
Planted: Quantity
Planted:

Date
Germinated: Quantity
Germinated:

Care
Instructions:

Known
Problems:

Projected
Height: Projected
Season Length:

How To
Harvest: Amount
Harvested:

Additional
Notes:

Plant Name: Description:

Date
Planted: Quantity
Planted:

Date
Germinated: Quantity
Germinated:

Care
Instructions:

Known
Problems:

Projected
Height: Projected
Season Length:

How To
Harvest: Amount
Harvested:

Additional
Notes:

PLANT PROFILE

Plant Name: _____   Description: _____

Date
Planted: _____   Quantity
Planted: _____

Date
Germinated: _____   Quantity
Germinated: _____

Care
Instructions: _____

Known
Problems: _____

Projected
Height: _____   Projected
Season Length: _____

How To
Harvest: _____   Amount
Harvested: _____

Additional
Notes: _____

SP
SPRING

Plant Name: _____   Description: _____

Date
Planted: _____   Quantity
Planted: _____

Date
Germinated: _____   Quantity
Germinated: _____

Care
Instructions: _____

Known
Problems: _____

Projected
Height: _____   Projected
Season Length: _____

How To
Harvest: _____   Amount
Harvested: _____

Additional
Notes: _____

PLANT PROFILE

Plant Name: Description:

Date
Planted: Quantity
Planted:

Date
Germinated: Quantity
Germinated:

Care
Instructions:

Known
Problems:

Projected
Height: Projected
Season Length:

How To
Harvest: Amount
Harvested:

Additional
Notes:

Plant Name: Description:

Date
Planted: Quantity
Planted:

Date
Germinated: Quantity
Germinated:

Care
Instructions:

Known
Problems:

Projected
Height: Projected
Season Length:

How To
Harvest: Amount
Harvested:

Additional
Notes:

Plant Name:

Description:

Date
Planted:

Quantity
Planted:

Date
Germinated:

Quantity
Germinated:

Care
Instructions:

Known
Problems:

Sp
SPRING

Projected
Height:

Projected
Season Length:

How To
Harvest:

Amount
Harvested:

Additional
Notes:

Plant Name:

Description:

Date
Planted:

Quantity
Planted:

Date
Germinated:

Quantity
Germinated:

Care
Instructions:

Known
Problems:

Projected
Height:

Projected
Season Length:

How To
Harvest:

Amount
Harvested:

Additional
Notes:

PLANT PROFILE

Plant Name: .... Description: ....

Date
Planted: ....

Quantity
Planted: ....

Date
Germinated: ....

Quantity
Germinated: ....

Care
Instructions: ....

Known
Problems: ....

Projected
Height: ....

Projected
Season Length: ....

How To
Harvest: ....

Amount
Harvested: ....

Additional
Notes: ....

Plant Name: .... Description: ....

Date
Planted: ....

Quantity
Planted: ....

Date
Germinated: ....

Quantity
Germinated: ....

Care
Instructions: ....

Known
Problems: ....

Projected
Height: ....

Projected
Season Length: ....

How To
Harvest: ....

Amount
Harvested: ....

Additional
Notes: ....

PLANT PROFILE

Plant Name: ....

Description: ....

Date
Planted: ....

Quantity
Planted: ....

Date
Germinated: ....

Quantity
Germinated: ....

Care
Instructions: ....

Known
Problems: ....

Projected
Height: ....

Projected
Season Length: ....

How To
Harvest: ....

Amount
Harvested: ....

Additional
Notes: ....

SP
SPRING

Plant Name: ....

Description: ....

Date
Planted: ....

Quantity
Planted: ....

Date
Germinated: ....

Quantity
Germinated: ....

Care
Instructions: ....

Known
Problems: ....

Projected
Height: ....

Projected
Season Length: ....

How To
Harvest: ....

Amount
Harvested: ....

Additional
Notes: ....

Notes:

Notes:

Notes:

Sp
SPRING

Notes:

GARDEN PLAN

GARDEN PLAN

GARDEN PLAN

SP
SPRING

GARDEN PLAN

GARDEN PLAN

SPRING TO DO LIST

○ _____ DATE

○ _____ DATE

○ _____ DATE

○ _____ DATE

○ _____ DATE

○ _____ DATE

○ _____ DATE

○ _____ DATE

○ _____ DATE

○ _____ DATE

○ _____ DATE

○ _____ DATE

○ _____ DATE

○ _____ DATE

○ _____ DATE

○ _____ DATE

○ _____ DATE

○   DATE

○   DATE

○   DATE

○   DATE

○   DATE

SP
SPRING

○   DATE

○   DATE

○   DATE

○   DATE

○   DATE

○   DATE

○   DATE

○   DATE

○   DATE

○   DATE

○   DATE

○   DATE

SPRING TO DO LIST

○   DATE

○   DATE

○   DATE

○   DATE

○   DATE

○   DATE

○   DATE

○   DATE

○   DATE

○   DATE

○   DATE

○   DATE

○   DATE

○   DATE

○   DATE

○   DATE

○   DATE

○   DATE

○   DATE

○   DATE

○   DATE

○   DATE

○   DATE

○   DATE

○   DATE

○   DATE

○   DATE

○   DATE

○   DATE

○   DATE

○   DATE

○   DATE

○   DATE

○   DATE

Sp

SPRING

MONTH / YEAR

SPRING

MONTH / YEAR

SPRING CALENDAR

MONTH / YEAR

SPRING CALENDAR

SPRING

SPRING CLIMATE DATA WORTH NOTING

DATE

DATE

DATE

DATE

DATE

DATE

DATE

DATE

DATE

DATE

DATE

DATE

Sp
SPRING

DATE

DATE

DATE

DATE

DATE

DATE

PESTS & PROBLEMS

DATE	PLANT	PROBLEM

PESTS & PROBLEMS

TREATMENT	DID IT WORK?

Go outdoors and look at the trees. See the specimens of foliage and new ones springing up all the while. Go in a garden and watch the flowers. It is just one principle – the principle is the same in every one, but see the enormous variety.

FRANK LLOYD WRIGHT

TALIESIN LANDSCAPE ABSTRACTION
EUGENE MASSELINK, 1935

Su

SUMMER

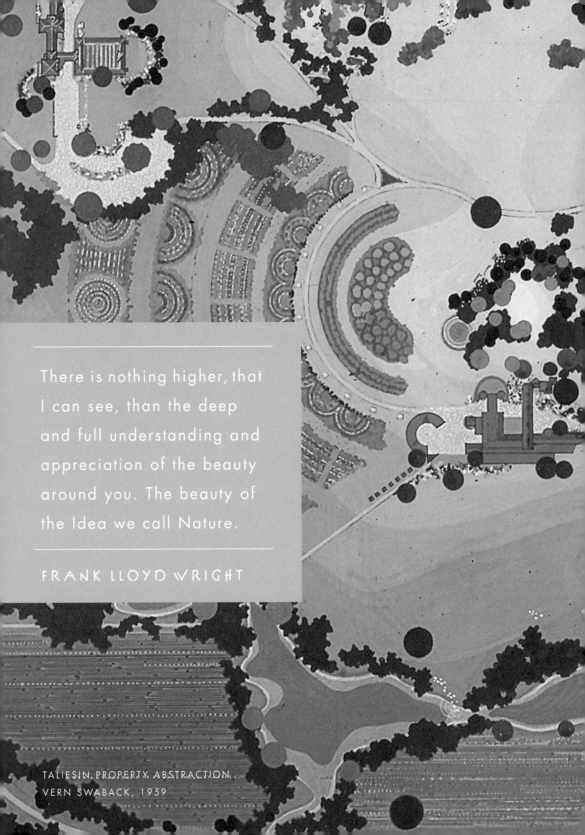

There is nothing higher, that
I can see, than the deep
and full understanding and
appreciation of the beauty
around you. The beauty of
the Idea we call Nature.

FRANK LLOYD WRIGHT

TALIESIN, PROPERTY ABSTRACTION,
VERN SWABACK, 1959

FERN ABSTRACTION
EUGENE MASSELINK

[If] you form the habit of nature
study, little by little you will
find your faculties strengthened,
refreshed, and capable of more
effective interpenetration, and
it will go on as long as you will.

FRANK LLOYD WRIGHT

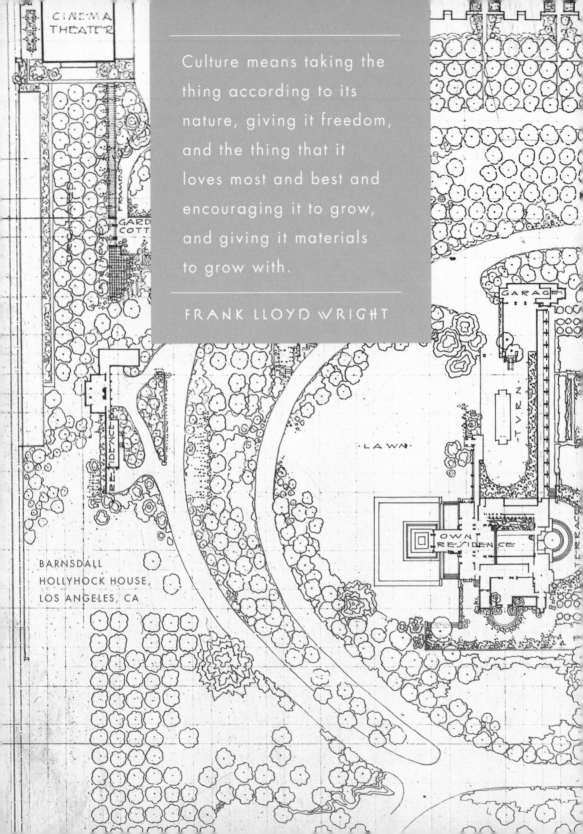

Culture means taking the thing according to its nature, giving it freedom, and the thing that it loves most and best and encouraging it to grow, and giving it materials to grow with.

FRANK LLOYD WRIGHT

BARNSDALL
HOLLYHOCK HOUSE,
LOS ANGELES, CA

PLANT PROFILE

Plant Name: Description:

Date
Planted: Quantity
Planted:

Date
Germinated: Quantity
Germinated:

Care
Instructions:

Known
Problems:

Projected
Height: Projected
Season Length:

How To
Harvest: Amount
Harvested:

Additional
Notes:

Plant Name: Description:

Date
Planted: Quantity
Planted:

Date
Germinated: Quantity
Germinated:

Care
Instructions:

Known
Problems:

Projected
Height: Projected
Season Length:

How To
Harvest: Amount
Harvested:

Additional
Notes:

PLANT PROFILE

Plant Name: Description:

Date
Planted: Quantity
Planted:

Date
Germinated: Quantity
Germinated:

Care
Instructions:

Known
Problems:

Projected
Height: Projected
Season Length:

How To
Harvest: Amount
Harvested:

Additional
Notes:

Su
SUMMER

Plant Name: Description:

Date
Planted: Quantity
Planted:

Date
Germinated: Quantity
Germinated:

Care
Instructions:

Known
Problems:

Projected
Height: Projected
Season Length:

How To
Harvest: Amount
Harvested:

Additional
Notes:

PLANT PROFILE

Plant Name: Description:

Date
Planted: Quantity
Planted:

Date
Germinated: Quantity
Germinated:

Care
Instructions:

Known
Problems:

Projected
Height: Projected
Season Length:

How To
Harvest: Amount
Harvested:

Additional
Notes:

Plant Name: Description:

Date
Planted: Quantity
Planted:

Date
Germinated: Quantity
Germinated:

Care
Instructions:

Known
Problems:

Projected
Height: Projected
Season Length:

How To
Harvest: Amount
Harvested:

Additional
Notes:

PLANT PROFILE

Plant Name: Description:

Date   Quantity
Planted: Planted:

Date   Quantity
Germinated: Germinated:

Care
Instructions:

Known
Problems:

Projected   Projected
Height: Season Length:

How To   Amount
Harvest: Harvested:

Additional
Notes:

Plant Name: Description:

Date   Quantity
Planted: Planted:

Date   Quantity
Germinated: Germinated:

Care
Instructions:

Known
Problems:

Projected   Projected
Height: Season Length:

How To   Amount
Harvest: Harvested:

Additional
Notes:

Su
SUMMER

PLANT PROFILE

Plant Name: Description:

Date
Planted: Quantity
Planted:

Date
Germinated: Quantity
Germinated:

Care
Instructions:

Known
Problems:

Projected
Height: Projected
Season Length:

How To
Harvest: Amount
Harvested:

Additional
Notes:

Plant Name: Description:

Date
Planted: Quantity
Planted:

Date
Germinated: Quantity
Germinated:

Care
Instructions:

Known
Problems:

Projected
Height: Projected
Season Length:

How To
Harvest: Amount
Harvested:

Additional
Notes:

PLANT PROFILE

Plant Name: Description:

Date
Planted: Quantity
Planted:

Date
Germinated: Quantity
Germinated:

Care
Instructions:

Known
Problems:

Projected
Height: Projected
Season Length:

How To
Harvest: Amount
Harvested:

Additional
Notes:

Su

SUMMER

Plant Name: Description:

Date
Planted: Quantity
Planted:

Date
Germinated: Quantity
Germinated:

Care
Instructions:

Known
Problems:

Projected
Height: Projected
Season Length:

How To
Harvest: Amount
Harvested:

Additional
Notes:

PLANT PROFILE

Plant Name:

Description:

Date
Planted:

Quantity
Planted:

Date
Germinated:

Quantity
Germinated:

Care
Instructions:

Known
Problems:

Projected
Height:

Projected
Season Length:

How To
Harvest:

Amount
Harvested:

Additional
Notes:

Plant Name:

Description:

Date
Planted:

Quantity
Planted:

Date
Germinated:

Quantity
Germinated:

Care
Instructions:

Known
Problems:

Projected
Height:

Projected
Season Length:

How To
Harvest:

Amount
Harvested:

Additional
Notes:

PLANT PROFILE

Plant Name: | Description:

Date
Planted: | Quantity
Planted:

Date
Germinated: | Quantity
Germinated:

Care
Instructions:

Known
Problems:

Projected
Height: | Projected
Season Length:

How To
Harvest: | Amount
Harvested:

Su
SUMMER

Additional
Notes:

Plant Name: | Description:

Date
Planted: | Quantity
Planted:

Date
Germinated: | Quantity
Germinated:

Care
Instructions:

Known
Problems:

Projected
Height: | Projected
Season Length:

How To
Harvest: | Amount
Harvested:

Additional
Notes:

Notes:

Su
SUMMER

Notes:

Notes:

Su
SUMMER

Notes:

GARDEN PLAN

Su
SUMMER

GARDEN PLAN

GARDEN PLAN

Su
SUMMER

GARDEN PLAN

Su

SUMMER TO DO LIST

○ _____ DATE _____

○ _____ DATE _____

○ _____ DATE _____

○ _____ DATE _____

○ _____ DATE _____

○ _____ DATE _____

○ _____ DATE _____

○ _____ DATE _____

○ _____ DATE _____

○ _____ DATE _____

○ _____ DATE _____

○ _____ DATE _____

○ _____ DATE _____

○ _____ DATE _____

○ _____ DATE _____

○ _____ DATE _____

○ _____ DATE _____

SUMMER TO DO LIST

○ _____ DATE

○ _____ DATE

○ _____ DATE

○ _____ DATE

○ _____ DATE

○ _____ DATE

○ _____ DATE

○ _____ DATE

○ _____ DATE

○ _____ DATE

○ _____ DATE

○ _____ DATE

○ _____ DATE

○ _____ DATE

○ _____ DATE

○ _____ DATE

○ _____ DATE

Su
SUMMER

SUMMER TO DO LIST

○   DATE

○   DATE

○   DATE

○   DATE

○   DATE

○   DATE

○   DATE

○   DATE

○   DATE

○   DATE

○   DATE

○   DATE

○   DATE

○   DATE

○   DATE

○   DATE

○   DATE

SUMMER TO DO LIST

○ _____ DATE

○ _____ DATE

○ _____ DATE

○ _____ DATE

○ _____ DATE

○ _____ DATE

○ _____ DATE

Su
SUMMER

○ _____ DATE

○ _____ DATE

○ _____ DATE

○ _____ DATE

○ _____ DATE

○ _____ DATE

○ _____ DATE

○ _____ DATE

○ _____ DATE

MONTH / YEAR

MONTH / YEAR

SUMMER CLIMATE DATA WORTH NOTING

DATE

DATE

DATE

DATE

DATE

DATE

DATE

DATE

DATE

SUMMER CLIMATE DATA WORTH NOTING

DATE

DATE

DATE

DATE

Su
SUMMER

DATE

DATE

DATE

DATE

DATE

PESTS & PROBLEMS

DATE	PLANT	PROBLEM

PESTS & PROBLEMS

TREATMENT	DID IT WORK?

Su
SUMMER

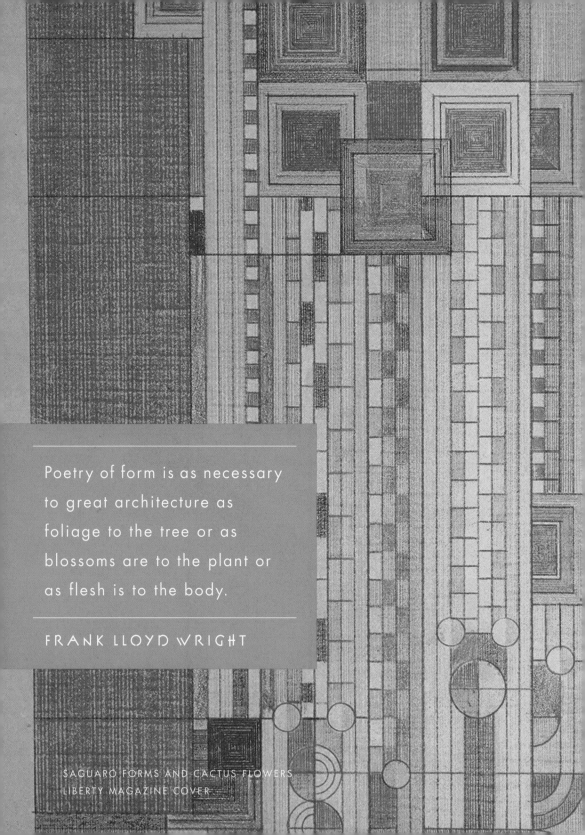

Poetry of form is as necessary
to great architecture as
foliage to the tree or as
blossoms are to the plant or
as flesh is to the body.

FRANK LLOYD WRIGHT

SAGUARO FORMS AND CACTUS FLOWERS
LIBERTY MAGAZINE COVER

F

FALL

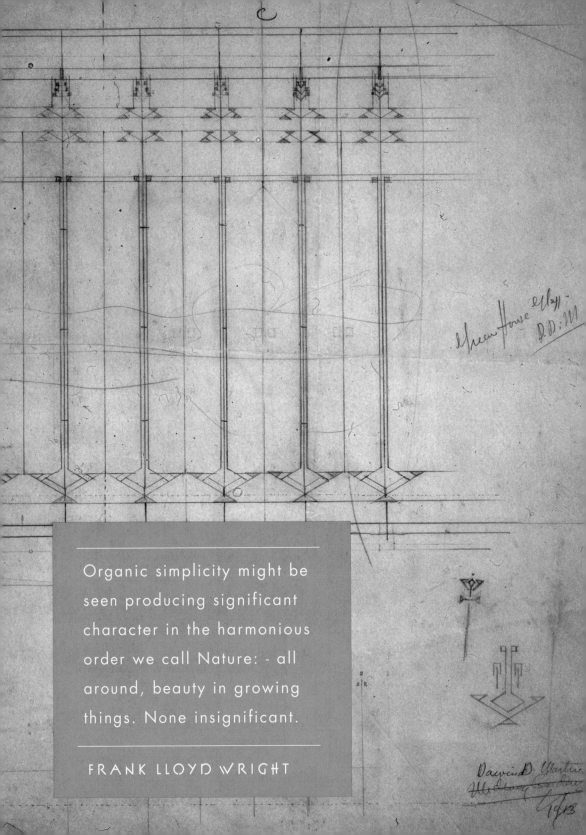

Organic simplicity might be seen producing significant character in the harmonious order we call Nature: - all around, beauty in growing things. None insignificant.

FRANK LLOYD WRIGHT

LEFT: MARTIN HOUSE ART GLASS WINDOW DRAWING

RIGHT: MARTIN HOUSE ART GLASS DOOR RENDERING

Look at the desert blooms,
you see all this great premium
placed upon individuality by
Nature. She loves it, insists
upon it, resists the loss of it.

FRANK LLOYD WRIGHT

F

TALIESIN WEST LANDSCAPE ABSTRACTION
VERN SWABACK, 1959

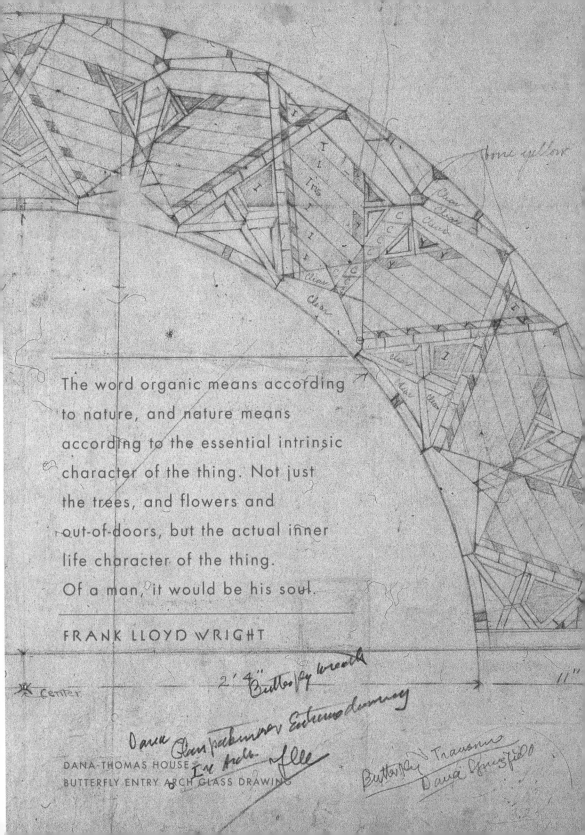

The word organic means according
to nature, and nature means
according to the essential intrinsic
character of the thing. Not just
the trees, and flowers and
out-of-doors, but the actual inner
life character of the thing.
Of a man, it would be his soul.

FRANK LLOYD WRIGHT

DANA-THOMAS HOUSE
BUTTERFLY ENTRY ARCH GLASS DRAWING

DANA-THOMAS HOUSE BUTTERFLY ENTRY ARCH GLASS
PHOTOGRAPH COPYRIGHT DOUG CARR
COURTESY OF THE DANA-THOMAS HOUSE FOUNDATION

PLANT PROFILE

Plant Name: Description:

Date   Quantity
Planted: Planted:

Date   Quantity
Germinated: Germinated:

Care
Instructions:

Known
Problems:

Projected   Projected
Height: Season Length:

How To   Amount
Harvest: Harvested:

Additional
Notes:

Plant Name: Description:

Date   Quantity
Planted: Planted:

Date   Quantity
Germinated: Germinated:

Care
Instructions:

Known
Problems:

Projected   Projected
Height: Season Length:

How To   Amount
Harvest: Harvested:

Additional
Notes:

PLANT PROFILE

Plant Name:

Description:

Date
Planted:

Quantity
Planted:

Date
Germinated:

Quantity
Germinated:

Care
Instructions:

Known
Problems:

Projected
Height:

Projected
Season Length:

How To
Harvest:

Amount
Harvested:

Additional
Notes:

F

FALL

Plant Name:

Description:

Date
Planted:

Quantity
Planted:

Date
Germinated:

Quantity
Germinated:

Care
Instructions:

Known
Problems:

Projected
Height:

Projected
Season Length:

How To
Harvest:

Amount
Harvested:

Additional
Notes:

PLANT PROFILE

Plant Name: Description:

Date
Planted: Quantity
Planted:

Date
Germinated: Quantity
Germinated:

Care
Instructions:

Known
Problems:

Projected
Height: Projected
Season Length:

How To
Harvest: Amount
Harvested:

Additional
Notes:

Plant Name: Description:

Date
Planted: Quantity
Planted:

Date
Germinated: Quantity
Germinated:

Care
Instructions:

Known
Problems:

Projected
Height: Projected
Season Length:

How To
Harvest: Amount
Harvested:

Additional
Notes:

PLANT PROFILE

Plant Name: Description:

Date
Planted: Quantity
Planted:

Date
Germinated: Quantity
Germinated:

Care
Instructions:

Known
Problems:

Projected
Height: Projected
Season Length:

How To
Harvest: Amount
Harvested:

Additional
Notes:

F

FALL

Plant Name: Description:

Date
Planted: Quantity
Planted:

Date
Germinated: Quantity
Germinated:

Care
Instructions:

Known
Problems:

Projected
Height: Projected
Season Length:

How To
Harvest: Amount
Harvested:

Additional
Notes:

PLANT PROFILE

Plant Name: Description:

Date
Planted: Quantity
                                     Planted:

Date
Germinated: Quantity
                                     Germinated:

Care
Instructions:

Known
Problems:

Projected   Projected
Height: Season Length:

How To   Amount
Harvest: Harvested:

Additional
Notes:

Plant Name: Description:

Date
Planted: Quantity
                                     Planted:

Date
Germinated: Quantity
                                     Germinated:

Care
Instructions:

Known
Problems:

Projected   Projected
Height: Season Length:

How To   Amount
Harvest: Harvested:

Additional
Notes:

PLANT PROFILE

Plant Name: Description:

Date
Planted:

Quantity
Planted:

Date
Germinated:

Quantity
Germinated:

Care
Instructions:

Known
Problems:

Projected
Height:

Projected
Season Length:

How To
Harvest:

Amount
Harvested:

Additional
Notes:

F

FALL

Plant Name: Description:

Date
Planted:

Quantity
Planted:

Date
Germinated:

Quantity
Germinated:

Care
Instructions:

Known
Problems:

Projected
Height:

Projected
Season Length:

How To
Harvest:

Amount
Harvested:

Additional
Notes:

PLANT PROFILE

Plant Name:

Description:

Date
Planted:

Quantity
Planted:

Date
Germinated:

Quantity
Germinated:

Care
Instructions:

Known
Problems:

Projected
Height:

Projected
Season Length:

How To
Harvest:

Amount
Harvested:

Additional
Notes:

Plant Name:

Description:

Date
Planted:

Quantity
Planted:

Date
Germinated:

Quantity
Germinated:

Care
Instructions:

Known
Problems:

Projected
Height:

Projected
Season Length:

How To
Harvest:

Amount
Harvested:

Additional
Notes:

PLANT PROFILE

Plant Name: Description:

Date   Quantity
Planted: Planted:

Date   Quantity
Germinated: Germinated:

Care
Instructions:

Known
Problems:

Projected   Projected
Height: Season Length:

How To   Amount
Harvest: Harvested:

Additional
Notes:

F

FALL

Plant Name: Description:

Date   Quantity
Planted: Planted:

Date   Quantity
Germinated: Germinated:

Care
Instructions:

Known
Problems:

Projected   Projected
Height: Season Length:

How To   Amount
Harvest: Harvested:

Additional
Notes:

Notes:

F

FALL

Notes:

Notes:

F

FALL

Notes:

GARDEN PLAN

GARDEN PLAN

F

FALL

GARDEN PLAN

GARDEN PLAN

GARDEN PLAN

GARDEN PLAN

FALL TO DO LIST

○   DATE

○   DATE

○   DATE

○   DATE

○   DATE

○   DATE

○   DATE

○   DATE

○   DATE

○   DATE

○   DATE

○   DATE

○   DATE

○   DATE

○   DATE

○   DATE

○   DATE

○   DATE

○   DATE

○   DATE

○   DATE

○   DATE

○   DATE

○   DATE

○   DATE

○   DATE

○   DATE

○   DATE

○   DATE

○   DATE

○   DATE

○   DATE

○   DATE

F

FALL

FALL TO DO LIST

○   DATE

○   DATE

○   DATE

○   DATE

○   DATE

○   DATE

○   DATE

○   DATE

○   DATE

○   DATE

○   DATE

○   DATE

○   DATE

○   DATE

○   DATE

○   DATE

FALL TO DO LIST

○   DATE

○   DATE

○ DATE

○ DATE

○ DATE

○ DATE

○ DATE

○ DATE

○ DATE

○ DATE

○ DATE

○ DATE

○ DATE

○ DATE

○ DATE

○ DATE

○ DATE

F

FALL

MONTH / YEAR

F

FALL

MONTH / YEAR

F

MONTH / YEAR

F

FALL

FALL CLIMATE DATA WORTH NOTING

DATE

DATE

DATE

DATE

DATE

DATE

DATE

DATE

DATE

DATE

DATE

DATE

DATE

F
FALL

DATE

DATE

DATE

DATE

DATE

PESTS & PROBLEMS

DATE	PLANT	PROBLEM

TREATMENT	DID IT WORK?

F

FALL